Start with English

3

English

D H Howe

Oxford University Press

Oxford University Press, Walton Street, Oxford OX2 6DP

OXFORD NEW YORK TORONTO
DELHI BOMBAY CALCUTTA MADRAS KARACHI
PETALING JAYA SINGAPORE HONG KONG TOKYO
NAIROBI DAR ES SALAAM CAPE TOWN
MELBOURNE AUCKLAND
and associated companies in
BERLIN IBADAN

OXFORD, OXFORD ENGLISH and the OXFORD ENGLISH logo
are trade marks of Oxford University Press

© Guided English Corporation 1978 and 1979
First published 1979
Twenty-second impression 1990

ISBN 0 19 433634 4

Illustrations by Jonnie Ata Mak

Printed in Hong Kong

NOTE TO THE TEACHER

Revision is a feature of **Book 3**. The first ten pages of the book are devoted to the revision of vocabulary and language structures taught in previous years. Throughout the book new items taught are revised systematically. There is also a good deal of 'built-in' revision, including the incidental revision of vocabulary in the phonic reading sections.

The year's work includes the following:

ORAL WORK   *Vocabulary*: A steady expansion of vocabulary now begins. The entire list is given at the end of the Teacher's Notes.

Language structure: A further 25 items are thoroughly taught and revised.

READING   The two approaches to reading—*Look and Say* and *phonics*—continue side by side. There is ample practice in reading sentences and groups of sentences, the oral use of which has already been mastered. Plentiful illustrations ensure that reading is meaningful. At the same time sounds associated with all except the most difficult letter combinations are dealt with one by one using as examples words that have been already taught orally, and with an illustration as a reminder of the meaning of the whole word whenever possible. This combination of *Look and Say* and systematic *phonics* should ensure that pupils are firmly on the road to reading accurately and fluently by the end of the year.

Revision

A: Look at Number 1. What is it?
B: It is an aeroplane.

1 aeroplane	2 cupboard	3 door	4 arm
5 shirt	6 eye	7 key	8 newspaper
9 pocket	10 baby	11 shop	12 window
13 picture	14 wheel	15 finger	16 ear
17 tick	18 foot	19 doll	20 mouth

Revision

1 house	2 teacher	3 leg	4 pupil
5 bus-driver	6 bicycle	7 policeman	8 cow
9 boy	10 cake	11 nose	12 girl
13 man	14 fly	15 postman	16 woman
17 road	18 face	19 handkerchief	20 hand
21 room	22 star	23 ice-cream	24 knee

1 A: Look at Number 1. Is it a pencil?

B: No, it is not. It is not a pencil.

A: Is it a house?

B: Yes, it is. It is a house.

2 A: Look at Number 2. Is he a policeman?

B: No, he is not. He is not a policeman.

A: Is he a teacher?

B: Yes, he is. He is a teacher.

Read and practise:

A: What is your name?

B: My name is Mimi.

A: Are you a girl?

B: Yes, I am. I am a girl.

A: Are you a boy?

B: No, I am not. I am not a boy.

A: What is your father's name?

B: His name is Mr. Bell.

A: Is that your book?

B: Yes, this is my book.

Revision

1 car	2 boat	3 bowl	4 bus
5 lamp	6 cake	7 telephone	8 spoon
9 umbrella	10 flower	11 ball	12 banana

1 A: Look at Number 1. What is this?

B: It is a car.

A: What colour is it?

B: It is blue. It is a blue car.

A: Where is the blue car?

B: It is under the green table.

2 A: Look at Number 1. Is there a car under the table?

B: Yes, there is. There is a car under the table.

Revision

1 glasses	2 bottles	3 boxes	4 clocks
5 cats	6 hens	7 oranges	8 pencils
9 matches	10 shoes	11 pens	12 pots

1 A: Look at Number 1. What are these?
   B: They are glasses.
   A: What colour are they?
   B: They are green. They are green glasses.
   A: Where are the green glasses?
   B: They are on the red table.

2 A: Look at Number 1.
       How many glasses are there on the table?
   B: There are four glasses on the table.

5

Revision

1 running	2 walking
3 standing	4 sitting
5 smiling	6 crying
7 eating	8 drinking
9 jumping	10 falling
11 pushing	12 pulling

1 A: Look at Number 1. Is he walking?

   B: No, he is not. He is not walking.

   A: What is he doing?

   B: He is running.

2 A: Look at Number 3. Are they sitting?

   B: No, they are not. They are not sitting.

   A: What are they doing?

   B: They are standing.

1 holding	2 walking	3 waiting	4 carrying
5 climbing	6 standing	7 drawing	8 riding

1 A: Look at Number 1. What is she doing?
   B: She is holding a book.

2 A: Look at Number 2. What is he doing?
   B: He is walking to the door.

3 A: Look at Number 3. What is she doing?
   B: She is waiting for a bus at a bus-stop.

Read and practise:

A: What are you doing?
B: I am holding my pencil.

Revision

1 John	2 Mary and Mimi	3 Peter
4 John and Mary	5 Miss Lee	6 Mr. Bell
7 Ann	8 Ann and Mary	9 Mimi
10 All the girls	11 Mr. Green	12 Tom
13 A dog	14 Peter	15 All the boys
16 All the boys		All the girls

1   A: Who has a red shirt?

       B: John has. He has a red shirt.

2   A: Who have blue dresses?

       B: Mary and Mimi have. They have blue dresses.

3   A: Who is kicking the ball?

       B: Peter is. He is kicking the ball.

Read and practise:

A:			
	Please	open close point at touch shut	the door. the window. your desk. your book. your eyes.

B:			
	I am	opening closing pointing at touching shutting	the door. the window. my desk. my book. my eyes.

Read the questions. Then say the answers.

1   What is your name?

2   Are you a boy?

3   Are you a girl?

4   What is your teacher's name?

5   How old are you?

6   What are you doing now?

7   What is there on your desk?

8   What are you holding in your hand?

9   What is your teacher holding in her hand?

10   What colour is your book?

11   What are your friends doing?

12   What is your teacher doing?

13   How many boys are there in the room?

14   How many girls are there in the room?

15   Where is the blackboard?

Read and practise:

What colour is	sugar? grass? salt? milk? ink?	Sugar Grass Salt Milk Ink	is	green. white. blue.

Unit I	**Uncountable nouns**	

1 This is a piece of chalk.

2 This is a piece of wood.

3 This is a piece of soap.

4 This is a piece of string.

5 This is a piece of paper.

6 This is a glass of water.

7 This is a bottle of milk.

8 This is a bowl of soup.

9 This is a bottle of ink.

10	This is a piece of chicken.
11	This is a piece of fish.
12	This is a tin of soup.
13	This is a packet of tea.

Practise questions and answers like these:

A: Look at Number 1. What is it?
B: It is a glass of milk.
A: Look at Number 2. What is it?
B: It is a piece of string.

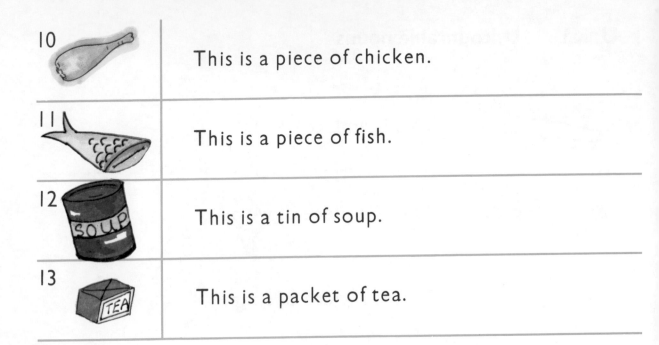

1 milk	2 string	3 ink	4 paper
5 water	6 chalk	7 sugar	8 coffee

1   Can she sing?
Yes, she can.

2   Can he sing?
No, he cannot.

3   Can she hear?
No, she cannot.

4   Can he hear?
Yes, he can.

5   Can he see?
No, he cannot.

6   Can he see?
Yes, he can.

7   Can she speak?
No, she cannot.

8

Can John swim?
Yes, he can.

9

Can Mimi cook?
No, she cannot.

10

Can Mr. Low drive a bus?
Yes, he can.

11

Can Mary ride a bicycle?
No, she cannot.

12

Can the men carry the box?
Yes, they can.

13

Can you see the bird in the tree?
Yes, I can.

14

Can you see the man in the sea?
Yes, I can.

1

I like apples.

2

I like oranges.

3

I like bananas.

4

I like sweets.

5

They like cakes.

6

They like ice-creams.

1

He likes the dog.

2

She likes the cat.

3

She likes the yellow flower.

4

He likes the red clock.

Revision

A Make six good sentences:

Please give me a	piece glass bottle bowl piece packet	of	water. chicken. soup. ink. tea. paper.

B Answer the questions:

1 Can a fish swim?
2 Can a cow fly?
3 Can a dog swim?
4 Can a cat swim?
5 Can you swim?

C Make five sentences beginning: I like...

D Make three sentences beginning: My friend likes...

1

Peter is tall but Mary is short.

2

This book is thick but this book is thin.

3

This writing is bad but this writing is good.

4

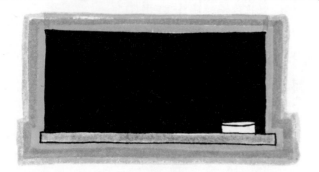 

This blackboard is black but this chalk is white.

1

Mary can swim but she cannot ride a bicycle.

2

Mimi can sing but she cannot cook.

3

The men can carry the box but they cannot carry the tree.

4

Mr. Low can drive a bus but he cannot fly an aeroplane.

Read:

1 This 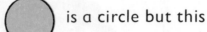 is a circle but this is not a circle. It is a square.

2 This is a bell but this 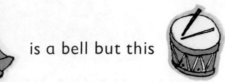 is not a bell. It is a drum.

3 This is a collar but this is not a collar. It is a tie.

4 He is a king but she is not a king. She is a queen.

5 This 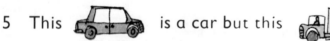 is a car but this is not a car. It is a lorry.

6 This is a pin but this is not a pin. It is a needle.

7 He  is a farmer but he is not a farmer.
He is a doctor.

8 This is a hammer but this is not a hammer. It is a nail.

Read aloud:

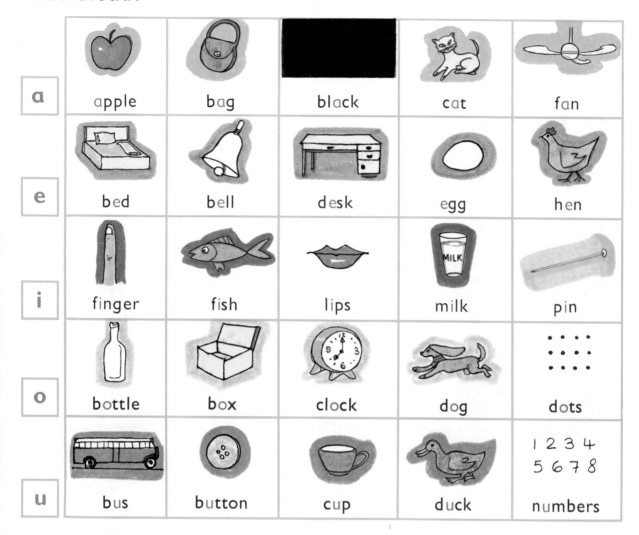

a	apple	bag	black	cat	fan
e	bed	bell	desk	egg	hen
i	finger	fish	lips	milk	pin
o	bottle	box	clock	dog	dots
u	bus	button	cup	duck	numbers

A rhyme to learn:

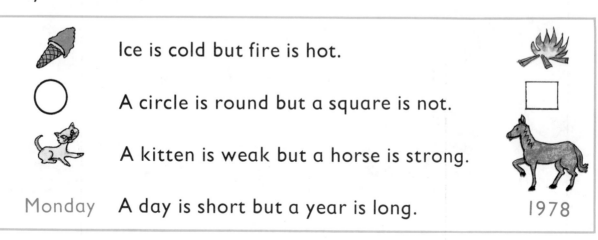

Ice is cold but fire is hot.

A circle is round but a square is not.

A kitten is weak but a horse is strong.

Monday   A day is short but a year is long.

Unit 5	That, Those

1

This is a pen and that is a pencil.

2

This is a bag and that is a box.

3

This is a book and that is a picture.

4

This is a flower and that is a tree.

5

This is a bird and that is an aeroplane.

1

These are glasses and those are bottles.

2

These are apples and those are oranges.

3

These are stockings and those are socks.

4

These are cats and those are dogs.

5

These are girls and those are boys.

1

 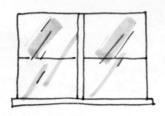

This window is open but that window is shut.

2

This bag is small but that bag is big.

3

This car is old but that car is new.

4

These apples are red but those apples are green.

5

These bottles are empty but those bottles are full.

1 Is this tea or coffee?

It is coffee.

2 Is this the top of the blackboard or the bottom?

It is the top of the blackboard.

3 Is this the back of the book or the front?

It is the front of the book.

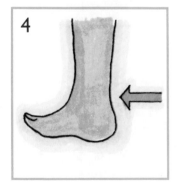

4 Is this an ankle or a knee?

It is an ankle.

Read and answer the questions:

1 Is that a bird or an aeroplane?

2 Is that the sun or a star?

3 Are those cars or lorries?

4 Are those pens or pencils?

5 Are those hats or coats?

1		Is this glass full or empty?
2	$\begin{array}{r} 298.765 \\ +\ \ 89.474 \\ \hline \hline \end{array}$	Is this sum easy or hard?
3	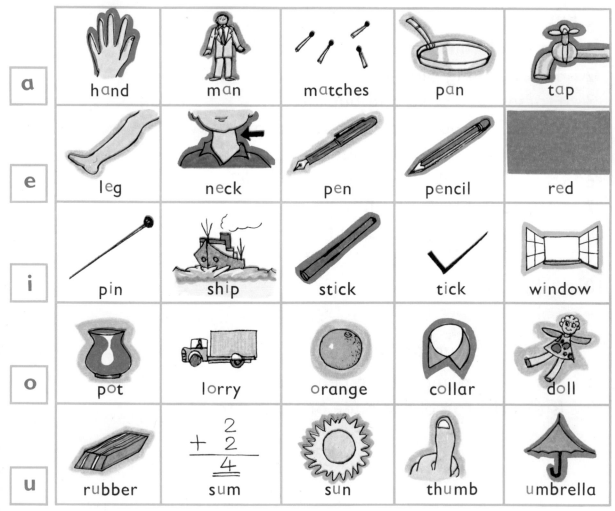	Is this shirt wet or dry?

Read aloud:

a	hand	man	matches	pan	tap
e	leg	neck	pen	pencil	red
i	pin	ship	stick	tick	window
o	pot	lorry	orange	collar	doll
u	rubber	sum	sun	thumb	umbrella

Revision

A   Answer the questions:

1   Is ice cold or hot?
2   Is water wet or dry?
3   Is a horse strong or weak?
4   Is walking easy or hard?
5   Is a pin small or big?
6   Is a page of a book thin or thick?

B   Put in is or are:

1   Ice is cold but fire _____ hot.
2   Trees are big but matches _____ small.
3   Horses _____ strong but kittens _____ weak.
4   We _____ boys but they _____ girls.
5   Collars _____ round but ties _____ not.
6   _____ a blackboard white or black?
7   _____ milk black or white?
8   _____ matches big or small?
9   _____ a year short or long?
10   _____ apples red or blue?

C   Answer the questions:

1   Are you writing with a pen or a pencil?
2   Is this the top of the page or the bottom?

Don't run.

Walk.

Don't sit on the desk.

Sit on the chair.

Don't write on the wall.

Write in your book.

Don't look at the window.

Look at the board.

Please don't walk on the grass.

Walk on the path.

Please don't walk in the street.

Walk on the pavement.

Please don't run across the road.

That is dangerous.

Please don't fight.

That is naughty.

1

Please be quiet.

Don't make a noise.

2

Please be careful.

Don't break the glasses.

3

Please be careful.

Don't be careless.

4

Please be quick.

Don't be late for school.

A rhyme to learn:

> Don't run across the road.
>   Stop and look.
> Don't write on the wall.
>   Write in your book.
> Don't run in school.
>   Always walk.
> Listen to the teacher.
>   Please don't talk.

Read aloud.   Make the sounds long.

a	p age	c ake	f ace	pl ate	d ate
i	f ire	n ine	l ine	sm ile	kn ife

o   st one   th ose   n ose   cl ose   h ome

u   r uler   use   J une

e   th ese

Unit 8	me, you, him, her, it, us, them

1

I am touching you.

You are touching me.

2

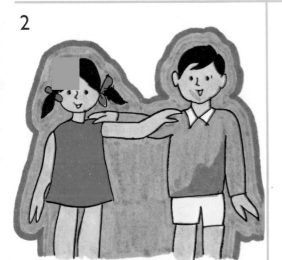

I am touching Mary.

I am touching her.

I am touching John.

I am touching him.

3

I am carrying a kitten.

I am carrying it.

1

Listen to me, children.

I am teaching you.

Yes, you are teaching us.

2

I am teaching the children.

I am teaching them.

How many sentences can you make?

He She	is	touching pointing at carrying holding talking to listening to	me. him. her. it. us. them.
You They	are		

Read and answer the questions:

1. Is Mary helping her mother?

Yes, she is. She is helping her.

2. Is John kicking the ball?

3. Is John catching the ball?

4. Is the dog playing with the children?

5. Are the children eating the oranges?

Read aloud:

| ea | = ee |

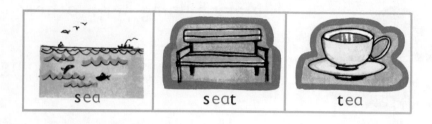

sea   seat   tea

read   easy   eat

speak   teach   clean

But: head   bread   breakfast

| **Revision** |

1   This is John. I am touching (him, her, it).

2   Miss Lee is talking. The children are listening to (him, her, it).

3   Don't open the door. Close (him, her, it).

4   The boys are listening. She is talking to (they, them, him).

5   We are listening to the teacher. She is talking to (we, her, us).

6   I am talking to the kitten. It is listening to (me, it, us).

1

This is a bucket.

This is a bucket, too.

2

This is a basin.

This is a basin, too.

3

This is a parcel.

This is a parcel, too.

4

This is a whistle.

This is a whistle, too.

5

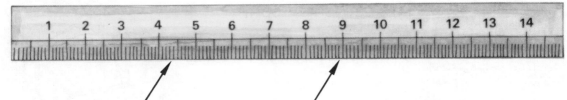

This is a centimetre and this is a centimetre too.

1
John is painting and
Peter is painting, too.

2
Mary is dancing and
Ann is dancing, too.

3
The boy is kneeling and
the girl is kneeling, too.

4
Mary is sewing and
Ann is sewing, too.

5
The cat is asleep and
the baby is asleep, too.

Peter Mary John Ann

Finish the sentences:

1 Peter's shirt is blue and John's shirt is blue, too.
2 Mary's dress is yellow and Ann's dress is ...
3 Peter's book is red and ...
4 Mary's basket ...
5 Peter's shoes are ...
6 Mary's shoes ...

Read aloud:

| oo (long) | moon | room | root | spoon | school |

too tooth

| oo (short) | book | cook | foot |

look good wood

1 She has a pen and I have one, too.

2 He has a book and I have one, too.

3 She is wearing a skirt and I am wearing one, too.

4

This letter has a stamp and this letter has one, too.

5

This house has a gate and this house has one, too.

41

These are ships.

This ship has a flag.

This ship has a flag, too.
It is the same one.

This ship has a flag, too.
It is a different one.

Read aloud:

| c | = s |

| face | pencil | ceiling | notice |
| circle | ice | dance | ice-cream |

42

Revision

Peter Mary John Ann

A Read:

1 Peter has a kite and John has one, too.
2 Mary has a kitten and Ann has one, too.
3 Peter's shirt is blue and John's shirt is blue, too.
4 Mary's skirt is red and Ann's skirt is red, too.
5 Peter's socks are red and John's socks are red, too.
6 Mary's socks are green and Ann's socks are green, too.

B Now make up
   sentences about
   May and Mimi.

May Mimi

Unit 11	**Adjectives**	

1
The cat is little.
It is a little cat.
It is not a big cat.

2
The woman is old.
She is an old woman.
She is not a young woman.

3
The dog is long.
It is a long dog.
It is not a short dog.

4
The boy is thin.
He is a thin boy.
He is not a fat boy.

5
The cat is dirty.
It is a dirty cat.
It is not a clean cat.

6
The man is unhappy.
He is an unhappy man.
He is not a happy man.

1	The yellow book is inside the big box.
2	The red book is inside the little box.
3	The red ball is in the yellow basket.
4	The blue book is on the green book.
5	The blue book is under the green book.
6	The blue book is behind the green book.
7	The green tree is beside the yellow house.
8	The green tree is near the yellow house.
9	The green tree is in front of the yellow house.

Read and answer the questions:

1. Is this a red flower or a yellow one?
It is a red one.

2. Is this a dirty shirt or a clean one?

3. Is he an old man or a young one?

4. Is this a big box or a small one?

5. Is this an old car or a new one?

6. Is this a white cat or a black one?

7. Is he a tall boy or a short one?

8. Is she a happy girl or an unhappy one?

9. Is this a small dog or a big one?

1

Boys, hold up your books.

We are holding up our books.

Look at the boys.

They are holding up their books.

2

Girls, hold up your rulers.

We are holding up our rulers.

Look at the girls.

They are holding up their rulers.

Read and answer the questions:

1 Look at the children.
   Where are their books?
   They are on their desks.
   Where are your books?
   Our books are on our desks.

2 Where are their rulers?
   Where are your rulers?

3 Where are their pens?
   Where are your pens?

4 What colour is their classroom door?
   What colour is your classroom door?

5 Look at the picture. Look at the dog.
   What colour is its head?

6 Look at the picture. Look at the cat.
   What colour is its tail?

Look at the dog.
Point to its tail.
Point to its head.
Point to its eyes.

Look at the cat.
Point to its tail.
Point to its head.
Point to its eyes.

Look at the cat and the dog.
Point to their tails.
Point to their heads.
Point to their eyes.

Read aloud:

 ar

car

star

arm

garden

hard   farm   mark   market

But: carry

1

Look at the doll.

Has it any legs?

Has it any arms?

It has some legs but it hasn't any arms.

2

Look at the man.

Has he any boxes?

Has he any books?

He has some boxes but he hasn't any books.

3

Look at the girl.

Is she wearing any socks?

Is she wearing any shoes?

She is wearing some shoes but she is not wearing any socks.

1 The doll hasn't any arms.

It has no arms.

2 The car hasn't any wheels.

It has no wheels.

3 The chair hasn't any legs.

It has no legs.

4 She hasn't any oranges.

She has no oranges.

5 They haven't any tails.

They have no tails.

6 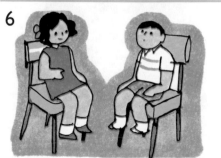 They haven't any desks.

They have no desks.

52

1

Do you want any flowers?

No, thank you.
I don't want any flowers.
I have a lot of flowers.

2

Do you want any bananas?

No, thank you.
I don't want any bananas.
I have a lot of bananas.

3

Do you want any kittens?

No, thank you.
I don't want any kittens.
I have a lot of kittens.

4

Do you want any pears?

No, thank you.
I don't want any pears.
I have a lot of pears.

How many?

1	He has a lot of books.
2	He hasn't many books.
3	He hasn't any books.
4	She has a lot of kittens.
5	She hasn't many kittens.
6	She hasn't any kittens.

Read aloud:

ai nail paint train tail rain

wait again

But: chair hair stairs

54

Revision

A Put in our, your, their or its:

  1 They are reading _____ books.
  2 We are writing in _____ books.
  3 John and Mary are sitting on _____ chairs.
  4 The dog is sitting on _____ tail.
  5 We are working in _____ classroom.

B Put in some, many or any:

  1 Mrs. Low has _____ apples but she hasn't _____ oranges.
  2 Mrs. Bell hasn't _____ pears but she has _____ bananas.
  3 Mary is wearing _____ shoes but she is not wearing
     _____ socks.
  4 Those cats have no tails. They haven't _____ tails.
  5 'Do you want _____ apples and oranges?'
     'I want _____ apples, please, but I don't want _____ oranges.
     I have _____ oranges.'

C Choose the true answer:

  1 Have you any brothers?   a. No, I haven't any brothers.
                                b. Yes, I have one brother.
                                c. Yes, I have some brothers.

  2 Have you any sisters?   a. No, I have no sisters.
                                  b. Yes, I have one sister.
                                  c. Yes, I have some sisters.

1

Is there any milk in the bottle?

Yes, there is some milk.

Is there any water in the bottle?

No, there isn't any water.

2

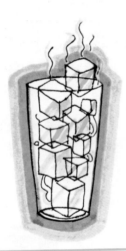

Is there any ice in the glass?

Yes, there is some ice.

Is there any ink in the glass?

No, there isn't any ink.

3

Is there any chalk in the box?

Yes, there is some chalk.

Is there any bread in the box?

No, there isn't any bread.

1 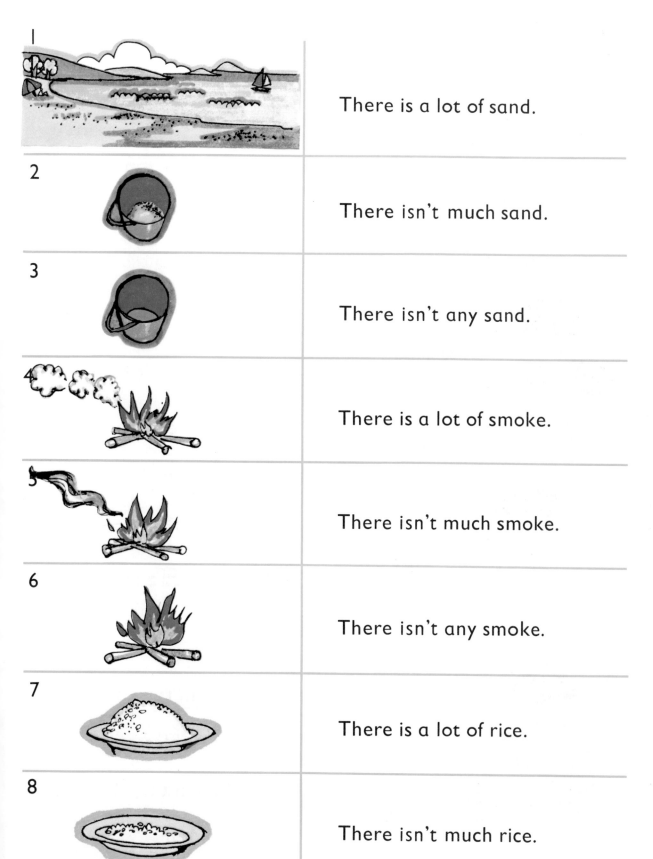	There is a lot of sand.
2	There isn't much sand.
3	There isn't any sand.
4	There is a lot of smoke.
5	There isn't much smoke.
6	There isn't any smoke.
7	There is a lot of rice.
8	There isn't much rice.

1

He has a lot of rice

but he hasn't much milk.

2

She has a lot of glasses

but she hasn't many cups.

3

He has a lot of chalk

but he hasn't much ink.

4

He has a lot of letters

but he hasn't many stamps.

1		There isn't any ink. There is no ink.
2		There isn't any milk. There is no milk.
3		There isn't any bread. There is no bread.
4		There isn't any rice. There is no rice.

Read aloud:

ow	brown	cow	down	how

town   towel   now

ow	throw	blow	bowl	show	yellow	window

ow	flower

1

Are there any flowers in the picture?

Yes, there are. There are some flowers.

2

Are there any flowers in the glass?

No, there aren't. There aren't any flowers.

3

Are there any people in the bus?

Yes, there are. There are some people.

4

Are there any people in the car?

No, there aren't. There aren't any people.

5

Are there any desks in your classroom?

Yes, there are. There are some desks.

6

Are there any cats in your classroom?

No, there aren't. There aren't any cats.

1 	Is there any water in the bucket? Yes, there is. There is some water.
2 	Are there any apples in the basket? Yes, there are. There are some apples.
3 	Is there any bread on the table? No, there isn't. There isn't any bread.
4 	Are there any plates on the table? No, there aren't. There aren't any plates.

Read aloud:

cloud	house	mouth	round	trousers

count   ground   loud   shout out   about

But: touch   colour   young

1

Are there any sweets in the bag?

No, there aren't any sweets but there is some money.

2

Are there any fish in the bowl?

No, there aren't any fish but there is some water.

3

Are there any apples on the plate?

No, there aren't any apples but there is some sugar.

4

Are there any books on the desk?

No, there aren't any books but there is some paper.

5

Are there any eggs in the bowl?

No, there aren't any eggs but there is some fruit.

1

Is there any water in the glass?

No, there isn't any water but there are some pencils.

2

Is there any food on the table?

No, there isn't any food but there are some knives and forks.

3

Is there any grass in the garden?

No, there isn't any grass but there are some flowers.

4

Is there any water in the boat?

No, there isn't any water but there are some men.

5

Is there any paper in the box?

No, there isn't any paper but there are some matches.

6

Is there any bread on the table?

No, there isn't any bread but there are some plates.

1

How many cakes are there in the cupboard?
How many cakes are there on the table?

There are a lot of cakes in the cupboard but there aren't many on the table.

2

How many flowers are there in the garden?
How many flowers are there by the road?

There are a lot of flowers in the garden but there aren't many by the road.

3

How many biscuits are there in the tin?
How many biscuits are there on the plate?

There are a lot of biscuits in the tin but there aren't many on the plate.

4

How many pictures are there on the wall?
How many pictures are there on the door?

There are a lot of pictures on the wall but there aren't many on the door.

1

How much water is there in the glass?
How much water is there in the bottle?

There is a lot of water in the glass
but there isn't much in the bottle.

2

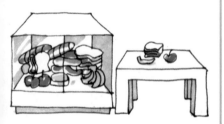

How much food is there in the
cupboard?
How much food is there on the table?

There is a lot of food in the cupboard
but there isn't much on the table.

3

How much bread is there in the basket?
How much bread is there on the plate?

There is a lot of bread in the basket
but there isn't much on the plate.

4

How much milk is there in the jug?
How much milk is there in the glass?

There is a lot of milk in the jug but
there isn't much in the glass.

Revision

A   Finish these sentences. They are about your classroom.

1   There are some desks in our classroom.
2   There aren't any . . .
3   There is some . . .
4   There isn't any . . .

5   There aren't many. . .
6   There isn't much . . .

B   Make up some sentences about your teacher's desk.
Use these words: books, pencils, cats, pens, chalk, ink, rice.
Example: There are some books on the teacher's desk.

C   What am I?

1   I have some legs but I haven't any arms.
What am I?   A table.
2   I have a mouth but I haven't any teeth.
What am I?   A river.
3   I have an eye but I haven't any ears.
What am I?   A needle.
4   I have a head but I haven't a neck.
What am I?   A nail or a pin.

1

It is time for school.
She is going to school.

Now she is at school.

2

It is time for work.
He is going to work.

Now he is at work.

3

It is time for bed.
He is going to bed.

Now he is in bed.

1

How are they going to school?

They are going on foot.

2

How are they going to school?

They are going to school by bus.

3

How is he going to work?

He is going to work by car.

4

How are they crossing the river?

They are crossing the river
by boat.

5

How are they going to the town?

They are going to the town
by train.

1

What is the box made of?

    It is made of wood.

What is it full of?

    It is full of chalk.

2

What is the glass made of?

    It is made of glass.

What is it full of?

    It is full of milk.

3

What is the tin made of?

    It is made of tin.

What is it full of?

    It is full of coffee.

A rhyme to learn:

Some people go to school by bus.

Some people go by train.

Some go by car, some go on foot,

but no one goes by plane.

1   What is your desk made of?
2   What is your pencil made of?
3   What is a bottle made of?
4   What is a tin made of?

Read aloud:

| o | = u |

money	months	colours	nothing

son	mother	brother	some

| above | Monday | another | |

Revision

Answer the questions:

Where is the girl going?

Where is the girl now?

Where is the boy going?

Where is the boy now?

What is the bottle full of?

What is the desk made of?

7   Can horses fly?

8   Can birds fly?

9   Can a bird read a book?

10   Can your teacher see you now?

Finish the sentences.

1	Mr. Low is going to work by _____ .
2	John is going to school on _____ .
3	These children are going to the town _____ .
4	These people are going home by _____ .
5	These children are going across the river by _____ .
6	Mr. Bell is going to England _____ .

May I go outside, please?

Yes, you may.

May I have an ice-cream, please?

Yes, you may.

Good morning, Miss Lee. May I carry your bag?
Good morning, Peter. Thank you. Yes, you may.

4

May I open a window, please?
> Yes, John. You may.

Ask your teacher:

May I	open the door, close the window, have a pencil,	please?

Now ask some different things.

Read aloud:

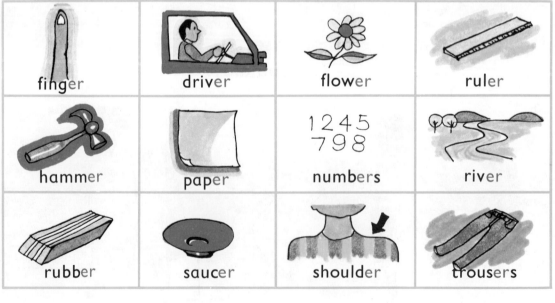

finger	driver	flower	ruler
hammer	paper	numbers	river
rubber	saucer	shoulder	trousers

| water | dinner | another | father |
| teacher | headmaster | letter | over |

74

1   He is a doctor.   a doctor

2   She is a nurse.   a nurse

3   He is a soldier.   a soldier

4   He is a sailor.   a sailor

5   He is a fruitseller.   a fruitseller

6   He is a gardener.   a gardener

7   He is a shopkeeper.   a shopkeeper

8   She is a servant.   a servant

1	He is a fisherman.	a fisherman
2	He is a workman.	a workman
3	He is a farmer.	a farmer
4	He is an engine-driver.	an engine-driver
5	He is a fireman.	a fireman
6	She is a pupil.	a pupil
7	He is a baker.	a baker

 1	He is a postman.	a postman
 2	He is a policeman.	a policeman
 3	She is a policewoman.	a policewoman
 4	He is a bus-driver.	a bus-driver

Read aloud:

 ir   girl    bird   shirt   skirt

 a dirty shirt   a dirty skirt

 ur   burn   turn   purse   nurse

Thursday   Saturday

Ask and answer questions like these:

a bus-driver?

Is he a bus-driver?

No, he isn't.

He is a farmer.

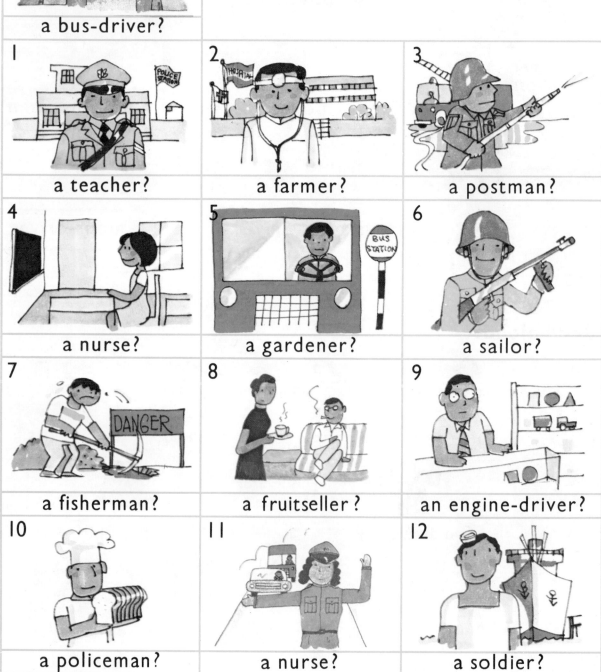

1. a teacher?
2. a farmer?
3. a postman?
4. a nurse?
5. a gardener?
6. a sailor?
7. a fisherman?
8. a fruitseller?
9. an engine-driver?
10. a policeman?
11. a nurse?
12. a soldier?

A   Put in am, is or are:

1   I am a doctor. I am working in a hospital.

2   I _____ a shopkeeper. I _____ working in a shop.

3   He _____ a fisherman. He _____ working in a boat.

4   She _____ a servant. She _____ working in a house.

5   They _____ sailors. They _____ working on a ship.

6   They _____ nurses. They _____ helping the doctor.

B   Put in has or have:

1   They are soldiers. They _____ guns.

2   He is a shopkeeper. He _____ a shop.

3   He is an engine-driver. He _____ an engine.

4   They are fishermen. They _____ boats.

5   He is a farmer. He _____ a farm.

C   Where can you see these?

| A fisherman | A teacher | A servant |
| A sailor | A shopkeeper | A nurse |

Unit 19	Comparison of adjectives

1

The boy is taller than the girl.

The girl is shorter than the boy.

2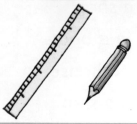

The ruler is longer than the pencil.

The pencil is shorter than the ruler.

3

The book is thicker than the newspaper.

The newspaper is thinner than the book

4

The tree is bigger than the flower.

The flower is smaller than the tree.

5

The man is stronger than the boy.

The boy is weaker than the man.

6

The apple is cheaper than the pear.

The pear is dearer than the apple.

1

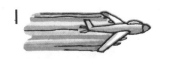

An aeroplane is faster than a car.

A car is slower than an aeroplane.

2

The yellow shirt is cleaner than the white one.

The white shirt is dirtier than the yellow one.

3

The girl is happy

      but the boy is happier.

4

The girl is greedy

      but the boy is greedier.

5

$$\begin{array}{r} 2 \\ +\ 2 \\ \hline 4 \end{array}$$

This sum is easy

      but this one is easier.

$$\begin{array}{r} 1 \\ +\ 1 \\ \hline 2 \end{array}$$

6

This stone is heavy

      but this one is heavier.

1

This face is ugly

    but this one is uglier.

2

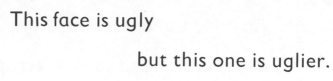

This picture is beautiful

   but this one is more beautiful.

3

This man is clever

   but this one is cleverer.

4

This is dangerous

   but this is more dangerous.

5

This boy is being careful

 but this one is being more careful.

6

This boy is being careless

but this one is being more careless.

1 $\frac{8}{10}$	This is good but this is better.	$\frac{9}{10}$
2 $\frac{1}{10}$	This is bad but this is worse.	$\frac{0}{10}$
3 a b c d e f g h i j	This writing is good but this is better.	a b c d e f g h i j
4 a b c d e f g h i j	This writing is bad but this is worse.	a b c d e f g h i j

Read aloud:

or   fork   forty   morning

or   for   short   story

But: **or** = er   doctor   sailor   scissors

Unit 20	**Here is ... Here are ...**	

1

Here is a piece of chalk.

Please draw a flower.

2

Here are some books.

Please put them on the desk.

3

Here is a duster.

Please clean the blackboard.

4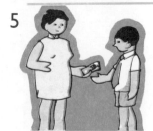

Here is a bandage.

Please tie it around my finger.

5

Here is some money.

Please buy some envelopes.

6

Here is a chain.

Please tie up the dog.

Teacher: Here is a pair of glasses.
          Are they your glasses, Mary?
Mary: Yes, Miss Lee. They are my glasses.
Children: Yes, Miss Lee. They are Mary's glasses.

Teacher: Here is a handkerchief.
          Is it your handkerchief, John?
John: Yes, Miss Lee. It is my handkerchief.
Children: Yes, Miss Lee. It is his handkerchief.

Read aloud:

| au |

saucer   daughter   naughty   August

Spring   Summer   Winter   Autumn

But: laugh

1

May I have some cotton, please?

Here it is!

2

May I have a piece of meat, please?

Here it is!

3

May I have a bag of flour, please?

FLOUR

Here it is!

4

May I have two blankets, please?

Here they are!

5

May I have some ripe apples, please?

Here they are!

6

That is 2.50, please.

Here it is!

Where is Mary?	There she is!
Where is Peter?	There he is!
Where is Ann?	There she is!
Where are John and Betty?	There they are!

Read aloud:

tr	 train	tree	trousers		
dr	 dress	drum	 drawer	 drinking	drive dry drawing
gr	 grass	green	grey	grandfather grandson grandmother grand-daughter	
br	 bread	brown	brush	breakfast brother bring	

1

Is there anything under the table?
Yes, there is.
There is something under the table.
It is a cat.

2

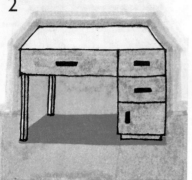

Is there anything under the desk?
No, there isn't.
There isn't anything under the desk.
There is nothing under the desk.

3

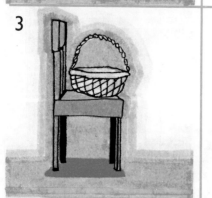

Is there anything on the chair?
Yes, there is.
There is something on the chair.
It is a basket.

4

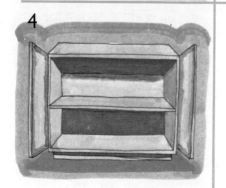

Is there anything in the cupboard?
No, there isn't.
There isn't anything in the cupboard.
There is nothing in the cupboard.

1   Is there anyone in the bus?

Yes, there is.

There is someone in the bus.

2   Is there anyone in the car?

No, there isn't.

There isn't anyone in the car.

There is no one in the car.

3   Is there anyone on the pavement?

Yes, there is.

There is someone on the pavement.

4   Is there anyone in the lorry?

No, there isn't.

There isn't anyone in the lorry.

There is no one in the lorry.

Ask questions about the pictures. Use anything or anyone.
Then answer the questions:

1. anyone
2. anything
3. anyone
4. anything
5. anything
6. anything
7. anyone
8. anyone

1   Is there anyone in the train?

No, there isn't.

There isn't anyone in the train.

There is no one in the train.

Read aloud:

-ng   ring   king   string   sing   song

wrong   bring   long   spring   thing

-nk   ink   drink   ankle   think   thank

90

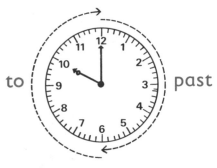

Look at the clock.

There are two hands,

a big one and a small one.

There are twelve hours.

There are sixty minutes.

What time is it?
It is ten o'clock.

It is twelve o'clock.

It is five past twelve.

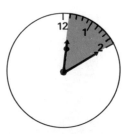

It is ten past twelve.

It is a quarter past twelve.

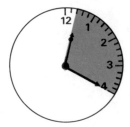

It is twenty past twelve.

It is twenty-five past twelve.

It is half past twelve.

It is twenty-five to one.

It is twenty to one.

It is a quarter to one.

It is ten to one.

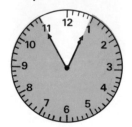

It is five to one.

Read aloud:

| fl | fly | flag | flower | flour | floor |

| cl | clock | cloud | clothes | clap | clever |

clean   class   climb   close

| pl | plate | playground |

add +; subtract −; multiply ×; divide ÷.

1 Start with one. **Add two. Subtract three.** Is there anything left?
2 Start with three. **Multiply by two. Subtract five.** Is there anything left?
3 Start with four. **Add six. Divide by two. Subtract five.** Is there anything left?

Revision

Look at your classroom and answer the questions:

1 Is there anyone in front of you?
2 Is there anyone behind you?
3 Is there anyone on your left?
4 Is there anyone on your right?
5 Is there anything on the blackboard?
6 Is there anything on the wall?
7 Is there anything on the desk?
8 Is there anything on the floor?
9 Is there anyone outside the classroom?
10 Is there anything in your right hand?
11 Is there anything in your left hand?
12 Is there anything in your pocket?

Ask and answer questions about the pictures:

1. What time is it?
   It is eight o'clock.
   It is time for breakfast.

Read aloud:

−le	bottle	circle	table	needle	whistle
	bicycle	handle	ankle	apple	little apple

1 	Where is the book? The book is on the desk. Put it on the chair.
2 	The book was on the desk. Now it is on the chair. Put it on the table.
3 	The book was on the chair. Now it is on the table.
1 	Where are the boys? They are in the tree.
2 	Where were the boys? They were in the tree. Where are the boys now? They are on the roof.
3 	Where were the boys? They were on the roof. Where are they now? They are in the car.

Revision

A   Answer Yes, I was or No, I was not:

   1   Were you in bed at five o'clock this morning?

   2   Were you in bed at eight o'clock this morning?

   3   Were you in school at seven o'clock this morning?

   4   Were you in school at nine o'clock this morning?

B   Answer Yes, they were or No, they were not:

   1   Were your friends in school at nine o'clock this morning?

   2   Were your friends in school at six o'clock this morning?

   3   Were your friends in school last Thursday?

   4   Were your friends in school last Sunday?

C   Answer Yes, it was or No, it was not:

   1   Was it Saturday yesterday?

   2   Was it a holiday yesterday?

   3   Was it a school day yesterday?

   4   Was it cold yesterday?

Finish the sentences:

1 Today is _____ day.
2 Yesterday was _____.
3 The day before yesterday _____ _____.
4 Three days ago it was _____.
5 Four days ago ____ _____ _____.
6 This year is 19 __ __.
7 Last year was 19 __ __.
8 The year before last _____ 19 __ __.
9 Ten years ago it _____ 19 __ __.
10 Last _____ day _____ a holiday.

Read aloud:

| sw | sweet | swim | switch | sweep |

| sm | smile | small | smell | smoke |

| sp | speak | spoon | **sl** | slow | sleep |

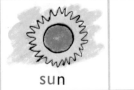

| su | sun | sum | subtract | summer |

But: sugar   Be careful with: school   scissors

1

John

> I had three apples
>
> but I was hungry.
>
> Now I have two.

2

Mary

Mary had five eggs

but she was careless.

Now she has four.

3

Tom

Tom had ten cakes

but he was greedy.

Now he has one.

4

Ann

Ann had three flowers

but she was careless.

Now she has two.

5

The men

The men had two boats

but there was a hole in one.

Now they have one.

Look at page **98**.

Did John have three apples?
Yes, he did. He had three apples.

Did Mary have six eggs?
No, she did not. She had five eggs.

Did Tom have ten cakes?
Yes, he did. He had ten cakes.

Did Ann have four flowers?
No, she did not. She had three flowers.

Did the men have two boats ?
Yes, they did. They had two boats.

Answer these questions:

1   How many apples did John have?
2   How many eggs did Mary have?
3   How many cakes did Tom have?
4   How many flowers did Ann have?
5   How many boats did the men have?

Give short answers:

1   Were you in school yesterday?

    Yes, I was or No, I was not.

2   Did you have any money in your pocket yesterday?

    Yes, I did or No, I did not.

3   Did the postman have a letter for you this morning?

4   Were your friends in school yesterday?

5   Did your teacher have white shoes yesterday?

6   Was your teacher in the classroom yesterday?

7   Did you have a cat in your desk yesterday?

8   Did your teacher have a piece of chalk yesterday?

Read aloud:

| **–rt** | shirt | short | skirt | start |

| **–rd** | bird | hard | word | cupboard |

| **–rn** | turn | learn | **–rm** | arm |

| **–rk** | mark | work | **–rl** | girl |

	first	second	third	fourth	fifth
1	short	very short	tall	very tall	not very
2	fat	very fat	thin	very thin	not very
3	small	very small	big	very big	not very
4	$\dfrac{8}{10}$ good	$\dfrac{10}{10}$ very good	$\dfrac{2}{10}$ bad	$\dfrac{0}{10}$ very bad	$\dfrac{5}{10}$ not very

1 The first boy is short.

The second boy is very short.

The third boy is tall.

The fourth boy is very tall.

The fifth is not very short and not very tall.

Now make sentences about the women in No. 2, the cars in No. 3 and the marks in No. 4.

A   Answer the questions:
1   Do you like school?   Yes, I like it very much.
2   Do you like sweets?   Yes, I like them very much.
3   Do you like snakes?   No, I don't like them.
4   Do you like bananas?
5   Do you like English?
6   Do you like Mathematics?
7   Do you like the radio?
8   Do you like your teacher?
9   Do you like dogs?
10 Do you like cats?

B   Make five sentences beginning: I like . . .
    Make five sentences beginning: I don't like . . .

C   Make sentences about these pictures:

| wet | hot | beautiful | big |

Read aloud:

| −11 | ball | bell | doll | all | tall |
| | fall | small | smell | kill | |

D Make sentences like these about the pictures below:

      1   The balloon is very small.

      2   The man is very old.

You may use any of these words. You may use some more than once:

small	old	long	brave	big	fast
greedy	clean	heavy	cold	short	happy
ugly	tall	wet	strong		

1 balloon	2 man	3 skirt	4 fireman	5 collar
6 car	7 boy	8 glass	9 bag	10 ice
11 nurse	12 sailor	13 face	14 soldier	15 man
16 workman	17 woman	18 hammer	19 hole	20 jug
21 kitten	22 parcel	23 packet	24 plane	25 girl

Revision

A Ask and answer questions like these:

What is this?
　　It is a piece of chalk.

What is this?
　　It is a plate of soup.

B Answer the questions:

1 Can you sing?　　Yes, I can.　　No, I cannot.
2 Can you swim?
3 Can you cook?
4 Can you see an aeroplane?
5 Can you hear an aeroplane?

C How many true sentences can you make? Use different words in the boxes.

I like $\boxed{?}$ but my $\left\{\begin{array}{l}\text{friend}\\\text{brother}\\\text{sister}\\\text{mother}\\\text{father}\end{array}\right\}$ likes $\boxed{?}$

D What are they saying?   The first two are done for you.

1
 This is a glass but that is a bottle.

2
 These are oranges but those are apples.

3

4
 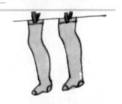

5

Revision

E   Ask and answer questions like these:

open? shut?

Is this window open or shut?
It is open.

red? green?

Are these books red or green?
They are green.

| 1 red? blue? | 2 big? small? | 3 fat? thin? | 4 full? empty? |
| 5 yellow? brown? | 6 white? black? | 7 tall? short? | 8 young? old? |

F   Put in the right words:
1   That is Tom. Can you see him?
2   There is Mary. Can you see _____?
3   There are a lot of people in the room. I can hear _____.
4   The teacher is saying something but I cannot hear _____.
5   We are behind the trees. No one can see _____.
6   Don't close the window. Please open _____.
7   I cannot see my dog. Can you see _____?
8   There is John. The teacher is talking to _____.

Revision

G Finish the sentences about the pictures:

John   Peter   Mary   Ann

1 John has a red hat and his shoes are red, too.
2 John has a blue shirt and . . .
3 Peter has a green hat and . . .
4 Peter has white socks and . . .
5 Mary has a blue skirt and her . . .
6 Mary has a white hat and . . .
7 Ann has a red skirt and . . .
8 Ann has yellow socks and . . .

9 John has a boat and Peter has one, too.
10 Peter has an aeroplane and . . .
11 Mary has a doll and . . .
12 Ann has a kitten . . .

H Put in my, your, its, our or their.

1 Look at the children. Can you see_____hats?
2 That cat is sitting on_____tail.
3 We work in this classroom. It is_____classroom.
4 'This is not my book. Is it your book?' 'Yes, it is.

It is_____book.'

Revision

1 Ask and answer questions about the pictures.

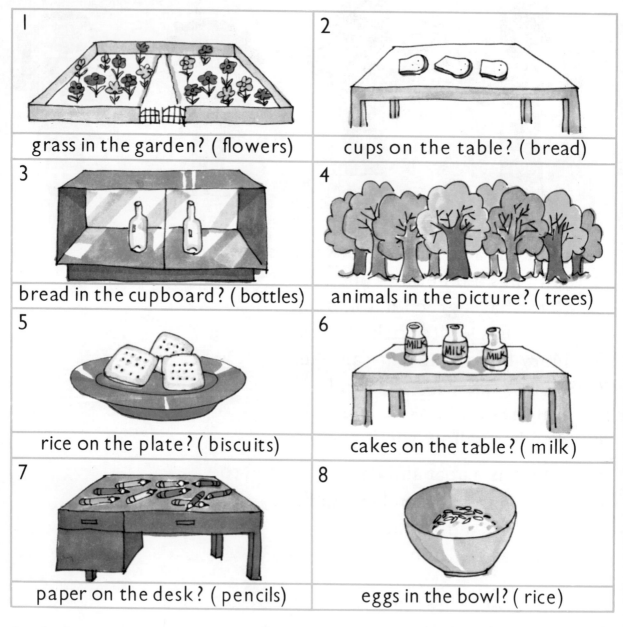

1 grass in the garden? (flowers)	2 cups on the table? (bread)
3 bread in the cupboard? (bottles)	4 animals in the picture? (trees)
5 rice on the plate? (biscuits)	6 cakes on the table? (milk)
7 paper on the desk? (pencils)	8 eggs in the bowl? (rice)

1 Is there any grass in the garden?
No, there isn't any grass in the garden but there are some flowers.

2 Are there any cups on the table?
No, there aren't any cups on the table but there is some bread.

Revision

J Ask and answer questions like these about the pictures on page 108:

1 Are there many flowers in the garden?
   Yes, there are. There are a lot of flowers in the garden.
2 Is there much bread on the table?
   No, there isn't. There isn't much bread on the table.
3 Are there many bottles in the cupboard?
   No, there aren't. There aren't many bottles in the cupboard.

K Read. Then answer the questions:

1

What is John?
   He is a pupil.
What time is it?
   It is eight o'clock.
   It is time for school.
Where is John going?
   He is going to school.

2

What is Mr. Lee?

What time is it?

Where is Mr. Lee going?

Revision

L Give answers like these:

1 Is a pencil longer than a ruler?   No, a pencil is shorter than a ruler.

2 Is a man shorter than a boy?   No, a man is taller than a boy.

3 Is a newspaper thicker than a book?
4 Is a man weaker than a boy?
5 Is a car faster than an aeroplane?
6 Is a girl taller than a woman?
7 Is a tree smaller than a flower?

M Ask and answer questions like these:

Is there anything in the bottle?
Yes, there is.
There is something in the bottle.
There is some milk.

Is there anyone in the room?
No, there isn't.
There isn't anyone in the room.
There is no one in the room.

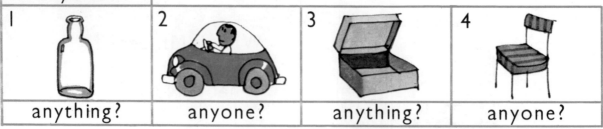

1	2	3	4
anything?	anyone?	anything?	anyone?

N What time is it?

Revision

O Add was, is, had or has.

1

1976   Now

In 1976 Mr. Low was a fisherman.
He had a boat.
Now he is a bus-driver.
He has a bus.

2

1973   Now

In 1973 Mr. Bell_____a soldier.
He_____a gun.
Now he_____a shopkeeper.
He_____a shop.

3

1975   Now

In 1975 Mr. Hall_____a postman.
He_____a bag.
Now he_____a farmer.
He_____a farm.

4

1969   Now

In 1969 Miss Rose_____ young.
She_____a bicycle.
Now she_____older.
She_____a car.

Revision

P Make sentences about the pictures like these:

John - tall

1974

Now

In 1974 John was tall.

Now he is very tall.

1 Miss Low - thin		2 Mrs. Bell - fat	
1975	Now	1973	Now
3 This car - old		4 Peter's shirt - dirty	
1960	Now	Yesterday	Now

Q Answer the questions:

1 Do you like sweets?

Yes, I like sweets very much.

or No, I don't like sweets very much.

2 Do you like chocolate?
3 Do you like school?
4 Do you like football?
5 Do you like picnics?